ZHENG HE

China's Greatest Navigator

ANDREW VIETZE

Published in 2018 by The Rosen Publishing Group, Inc.
29 East 21st Street, New York, NY 10010

First Edition

Library of Congress Cataloging-in-Publication Data

Names: Vietze, Andrew, author.
Title: Zheng He : China's greatest navigator / Andrew Vietze.
Other titles: China's greatest navigator
Description: First edition. | New York : Rosen Publishing, [2018] | Series: Spotlight on explorers and colonization | Includes bibliographical references and index.
Identifiers: LCCN 2017003224| ISBN 9781508175094 (library-bound) | ISBN 9781508175070 (pbk.) | ISBN 9781508175087 (6-pack)
Subjects: LCSH: Zheng, He, 1371–1435—Travel—Juvenile literature. | Explorers—China—Biography—Juvenile literature. | Discoveries in geography—Chinese—Juvenile literature.
Classification: LCC DS753.6.Z47 V54 2017 | DDC 910.92 [B]—dc23
LC record available at https://lccn.loc.gov/2017003224

Manufactured in the United States of America

CONTENTS

ARMADA FOR THE AGES

Almost a century before Christopher Columbus journeyed west looking for a route to Asia, Admiral Zheng He sailed more than 35,000 miles (56,327 kilometers) from his home in China. He led the largest fleet of ships the world had ever seen on a series of seven epic adventures. The ships traveled from China to India, Africa, and the Middle East. Known as the Treasure Fleet, the great armada was made up of the biggest wooden ships to ever sail.

Zheng He battled pirates, met with kings, and made diplomatic ties. He expanded trade and brought Chinese culture to foreign ports.

The admiral Zheng He was China's greatest explorer. He was little known in the West until recent years, but his accomplishments are being recognized widely now.

He even traveled to India almost a hundred years before the Portuguese visited China by sea. More than that, Zheng He introduced new religions and new technologies, founded colonies, and expanded Chinese influence. His crew kept detailed notes, giving historians an idea of life across the globe. In doing so, Zheng He and his giant navy changed the very face of the world.

AN ADMIRAL IS BORN

Zheng He was born in a small Muslim village in Yunnan Province in southwest China around 1371. When he was a boy, he was known as Ma He. His family descended from Chinese as well as Persian ancestors. The Persian immigrants moved to China with the Mongols under Genghis Khan. Young Ma He grew up in the foothills of the mighty Himalayas, thousands of miles from the sea. His family were Muslims, followers of Islam and the prophet Muhammad. They were a small minority in China at the time.

When Ma He was about ten years old, the Chinese invaded Yunnan, which was in the

Famous as a seafarer, Zheng He was born far inland, in the shadow of the Himalayas, the world's highest mountains.

control of the Mongols. Ma He's father was killed during the battle, and Ma He was taken prisoner by the Chinese. He was castrated, which the Chinese did because they thought it weakened men. Eunuchs, they believed, could be trusted in their households as servants.

THE YONGLE EMPEROR

Ma He impressed his captors with his intelligence and bravery. They sent him to work as a personal servant to Prince Zhu Di. The emperor's fourth son, Zhu Di lived in Beijing, near China's northern border. The prince liked young Ma He and made sure the young boy was given a good education.

Ma He grew to be massive. Old histories claim he was almost seven feet tall. He was a great ally for prince Zhu Di. The pair fought side by side during battles against the Mongols. When Zhu Di rebelled against the emperor, Ma He was with him. Zhu Di eventually grabbed power, becoming known as the Yongle Emperor. *Yongle* means "perpetual happiness." Zhu Di rewarded his loyal servant, making Ma He grand director, a position of great power. And he changed his name to Zheng He.

THE TREASURE FLEET

In 1403, the Yongle Emperor decided to expand his influence outside of China. He put more than twenty-thousand shipwrights, carpenters, sailmakers, loggers, and craftsmen to work building ships. The result was a fleet of the largest wooden vessels ever built. The ships were longer than football fields. They reached four stories tall, with dragon eyes on the bow.

Almost like floating towns, they carried more than five hundred passengers each. On board were sailors, soldiers, navigators, cooks, priests, doctors, and diplomats.

Zheng He's Treasure Fleet was the largest armada the world would see until the American navy of World War II, more than five hundred years later.

Scribes also joined them to write about every place they visited.

Each ship was a marvel of technology for the day. The Chinese were the first to use rudders, single masts, watertight compartments, and square sails. Many ships were filled with crafts, gifts, and tributes to give to the kings, queens, and other royalty they would visit. The giant armada was called the Treasure Fleet.

THE WORLD'S LARGEST NAVY

In the autumn of 1405, the Treasure Fleet was ready. The Yongle Emperor placed Zheng He in command of the largest navy the world had ever known. It included 317 ships carrying about twenty-eight thousand men. The emperor named Zheng He "Admiral of the Western Seas" and gave him several tasks. He was to bring gifts to leaders of other nations, show them China's power, and expand trade.

The massive vessels dwarfed most ships of the time. Zheng He's flagship, for example, was about 400 feet long (122 meters). This was six times bigger than Christopher Columbus's *Santa Maria*. The flotilla included

Zheng He's ships were massive, and they became legendary in China, as this stamp from 1991 shows.

troop ships, warships, water tankers, supply ships, horse carriers, repair vessels, patrol boats, and the treasure boats.

Before setting sail, Zheng He prayed to the goddess of the sea. He asked her to bless his journey. Huge crowds sang and cheered as the ships' red silk sails unfurled. The long procession got underway on the Yangtze River.

THE FIRST VOYAGE

The Treasure Fleet sailed south for days along the coast of China. Its first official stop was in Champa, a long, wide peninsula that stretches south from mainland China. Today, it is the country of Vietnam. When Zheng He and the Treasure Fleet approached Champa, the shores quickly lined with soldiers ready to attack them. Zheng He was quick to point out that they came in peace, bearing gifts from the Chinese emperor. The king of Champa ordered his men to put down their weapons, and he welcomed the Chinese admiral.

One of Zheng He's first stops was Champa, a kingdom on the coast of what is now southern Vietnam.

Zheng He and his men were offered a tour of the kingdom. They exchanged gifts and tributes with the king. Together, the group feasted for days. China added Champa to its list of friends. The small state would become a trading partner that was visited by the Treasure Fleet many times.

PIRATES!

Zheng He's mission was one of peace, as he told the king of Champa. But the fleet did include many warships with thousands of soldiers aboard, just in case. The Chinese were ahead of their time when it came to fighting. They had invented gunpowder and used the explosive long before any other culture. More than three hundred different weapons were on board the Treasure Fleet. These included cannons, flaming arrows, and small bombs, along with swords and knives.

Zheng He himself had years of experience in military campaigns. When he heard about a pirate named Chen Zuyi, who was

The Chinese were the first to use gunpowder, and their artillery, like this fifteenth-century cannon, gave them a huge advantage over their enemies.

menacing ships and bullying the prince of Malacca, he vowed to do something about it. The Treasure Fleet and Chen Zuyi's flotilla of pirate ships fought a fierce battle. Zheng He won, capturing Chen Zuyi and his men and destroying his fleet of ships.

WE SAIL AGAIN

Zheng He's first voyage took him from China all the way to Calicut, India. Over the course of two years, his vast navy visited many exotic ports of call in between—Java, Ceylon, Sumatra, and Malacca. Some say Zheng He was the first Chinese sailor to cross the Indian Ocean, but this is unlikely. When the fleet reached the horn of the Indian Peninsula, Zheng He decided to turn for home.

Everywhere they went, Zheng He and his men exchanged gifts and information with foreign leaders. They invited many on board to return to China to meet the emperor and

The massive fleet of Zheng He paid official visits to many colorful and exotic ports, including Java, in what is now Indonesia.

set up diplomatic relations. After these rulers and ambassadors pledged allegiance to the emperor, the Treasure Fleet brought them home. Zheng He unloaded the treasures and tributes he took in on his first trip and made ready for another voyage. He would take all these guests back to their kingdoms and collect more treasure.

THE SECOND TIME AROUND

The next year, in 1407, the Treasure Fleet sailed again, this time with 249 ships. On board were the ambassadors Zheng He had picked up on his first voyage. The second cruise was much like the first, stopping at most of the same places to let off passengers.

Zheng He had learned what many kings and princes liked during his previous trip. He filled his ships with porcelain plates, cups and vases, silk, iron, gold, silver, salt, books, candles, gems, and other items. He knew this would gain the favor of the rulers of foreign lands—and win their allegiance for China.

The second voyage succeeded at firming up relationships built during the first voyage.

Once again, Zheng He made it as far as India before turning around and sailing for home. China now had many trading partners on the Indian Ocean and access to a whole world of goods.

WAR

On his first visit to Ceylon, today's Sri Lanka, Zheng He was threatened and treated badly by the king. He decided to sail away rather than fight. But he heard later that the king of Ceylon was bullying neighboring countries, too. Zheng He decided to put a stop to the bullying.

When the Treasure Fleet sailed for the third time in 1409, Zheng He stopped by Ceylon and again was mistreated. This time he mounted an attack. It was the only major land campaign undertaken during the Treasure Fleet's voyages and the biggest event during the third voyage.

Known today as Sri Lanka, Ceylon was a center of Buddhist learning, and it was the site of the only major land battle mounted by Zheng He during his famous expeditions.

Zheng He defeated the king of Ceylon using his sea power and skills he learned fighting the Mongols. The result was a rout of the Ceylon troops. He captured the Ceylon king and took him back to China. The emperor spared the king and even gave him gifts before sending him back home.

ACROSS THE ARABIAN SEA

Zheng He's first three journeys took him across the Indian Ocean to mainland India. The emperor ordered Zheng He to push west even farther. On his fourth trip, in 1413, the admiral sailed farther than ever before, following the winds to the port of Hormuz.

An ancient city on the Persian Gulf, where Iran is today, Hormuz was a trading center. There, goods from Africa, the Middle East, India, and China all changed hands. The city was famous for its precious jewels, and the emperor of China wanted pearls, rubies, and diamonds. Zheng He arranged to buy as many as he could.

Some historians believe this fifteenth-century map of the world was compiled by Zheng He.

As a Muslim, the admiral was intrigued to see so many other worshippers of Islam. By the end of the fourth expedition, eighteen different kingdoms sent tribute to the Chinese emperor, an example of the expanding influence of China.

TO AFRICA

Some historians think Zheng He's fifth journey in 1417 was more about discovery than diplomacy. The Chinese had little contact with Africa. They had heard of lands beyond India from merchants traveling along the Silk Road. But the continent was new to them.

Zheng He's men found Swahili, in southeast Africa, a wonder to behold. They also spent months traveling down the east coast, stopping at Mogadishu, Brava, and Malindi. They marveled at how the Africans lived. Zheng He's scribes wrote about how people would "pile up stones to make their dwellings." Some Africans were intimidated by the size of the Treasure Fleet. But others welcomed the visitors with open arms.

Zheng He and his men were fascinated by the landscape and lifestyle of the people of Malindi, a port in today's Kenya, and other places on Africa's Swahili coast.

Zheng He filled his ships with more treasure. In Malindi, the Treasure Fleet even took on board an animal their hosts called a unicorn. The Somali word for "giraffe" sounds similar to the Chinese pronunciation of "unicorn."

LIONS, ZEBRAS, AND GIRAFFES

The Malindi people offered Zheng He a giraffe in tribute. Having never seen such a creature, many Chinese thought it actually was the exotic, legendary unicorn. They were in awe of the towering animal.

Zheng He took in an array of beautiful creatures. The Treasure Fleet became a floating zoo with lions, zebras, ostriches, leopards, and, of course, the giraffe. The ruler of Malindi wanted to present all of these to the emperor himself. He came aboard the ship with Zheng He.

When they returned to China, the Yongle Emperor was well pleased with the gifts. He was especially happy about the giraffe. As

The Chinese were astonished when Zheng He brought a *quilin*, a mythical creature like a unicorn, back to China. It was really an African giraffe.

legend has it, the unicorn was thought to appear when the world was in harmony. The Chinese felt that the gift of the giraffe was proof that the emperor of China ruled with the blessing of heaven.

THE FORBIDDEN CITY

As the voyages of the Treasure Fleet demonstrate, the Yongle Emperor was eager to show the world his power. He decided to move the capital of China from Nanjing to Beijing. There he built an imperial palace that would be a showplace to the world. Not only did the emperor want a huge estate that would impress visitors, he wanted it filled with riches and treasure.

Construction began in 1406, with more than a million loggers, carpenters, masons, and laborers working around the clock. In 1420, the Forbidden City was opened. It was given its name because everyone was forbidden to enter unless invited by the emperor.

Besides Zheng He's travels, the Yongle Emperor's most famous accomplishment was building the Forbidden City, an imperial palace of 8,704 rooms.

Ambassadors from around the world came to see the palace, many arriving on Zheng He's ships. China's famous Forbidden City would be the seat of power for the next five hundred years. Today, it is among the world's most-visited places.

THE DIVINE LAMP

On one of its last voyages, while returning to China, the Treasure Fleet was hit by a violent storm. Waves pounded Zheng He's ship. Even though it was 400 feet (122 m) long, it was tossed around like a bathtub toy. Several men were lost as they were washed into the sea. Everyone thought that evil sea dragons had caught them and were going to pull them under.

Legend has it Zheng He prayed to Tianfei, goddess of the sea. Not long after, rays of light beamed down from the sky onto his ship. Zheng He later called the light a "divine lamp." The wind had vanished, and the seas calmed. The fleet was safe.

A swirl of electricity like lightning, St. Elmo's fire seemed like magic to Zheng He, but it is really a simple scientific phenomenon.

Scientists today believe Zheng He saw St. Elmo's fire, a glow given off by objects during rare lightning storms. Zheng He was convinced his prayers were answered by Tianfei. When he returned to China, he built a temple in her honor.

CARVED IN STONE

At several places during his famous travels, Zheng He had stone tablets erected to commemorate his voyages. He left one at Calicut, describing the similarities between the people of India and the people of China. Another was placed in Cochin, in today's India, singing the praises of the emperor and his power.

Before he left for what would be his final voyage, Zheng He had two other stones placed in the Chinese towns of Changle and Liujiagang. These were to set in stone his own legacy. They listed the dates of each voyage and provided other details of his travels.

This is a replica of the stele—or stone monument—erected by Zheng He in Sri Lanka in 1409 to honor the gods.

The tablets proudly describe Zheng He's "unifying seas and continents." They boast how countries "beyond the horizon from the ends of the earth" had become subjects of the Chinese crown. And they praise the scientific advances made by Zheng He, in cartography and geography.

DEATH OF AN EMPEROR

In 1424, the Chinese battled the Tartars, a Turkic people, on their western border. The Yongle Emperor traveled with the troops to subdue them. On his way back to Beijing, he died. The new emperor, Zhu Di's son, issued his very first order: the Treasure Fleet was to be decommissioned.

The new emperor wanted to limit the spending of funds on unnecessary exploring. He called back Chinese ambassadors from all foreign lands. He banned further travel. Instead of making alliances and gathering treasure on the seas, he wanted his people working at home.

Zheng He served under several occupants of the Dragon Throne, the seat of Chinese power in the Imperial Palace.

Zheng He was to report to Nanjing, where he would serve as the military commander of an army station. For more than six years, Zheng He's great armada sat at the dock. Eventually, the emperor died and another ascended the Dragon Throne. This emperor sent Zheng He back to the ships with an order to get them ready for the greatest journey of them all.

DISTANT LANDS BEYOND THE SEAS

Zheng He's final orders were to sail beyond the known world. In 1432, he was told to inform the rulers of "distant lands beyond the seas" about the new Chinese emperor.

Zheng He was again put in command of a massive fleet—more than three hundred vessels and some twenty-seven thousand men. They retraced the route that they had sailed so many times. They stopped in Champa, Malacca, Sri Lanka, Hormuz, and Malindi, visiting their friends. They even traveled to Saudi Arabia and Oman,

Zheng He's famous journeys began in Nanjing, and that's where they ended for the legendary admiral, who is memorialized at this tomb in the maritime city.

spreading the word about the new emperor and taking in treasure and tribute.

Historians believe some members of the fleet even went overland to see Mecca, the holy city of Islam. But Zheng He was not among them. He took ill on the voyage and died on the way home. A memorial was built in his honor in Nanjing. People still visit there today.

THE LEGEND GROWS

Zheng He left a lasting legacy. His voyages were of a scale that the world had never seen. He was admiral of the largest ships in the biggest armada to ever have been assembled. He traveled more than 35,000 miles (56,327 km)—a distance that could have circled the globe.

Some historians believe that Zheng He actually did sail around the world, even making it as far as America. If so, the voyage would have taken place sixty years before Columbus, but that has never been proven.

Zheng He's voyages shared Chinese advances in navigation, cartography, shipbuilding, and gunpowder with other

Zheng He is remembered fondly not just in China but in many of the places he visited, including Malacca, part of today's Malaysia.

places. They spread the word of Islam, Buddhism, and other Chinese religions. They made allegiances for China and vastly expanded Chinese trade. Zheng He's scribes recorded all the places they visited, creating priceless historical documents. And like the Silk Road, all this activity opened up China, one of the world's most closed societies, to the wider world.

GLOSSARY

admiral A navy leader.

allegiance A friendship between two entities.

ambassador The official representative from one nation to another.

armada A fleet of ships.

Buddhism A way of life that follows the teachings of the Buddha, a prophet from India.

castrate The act of removing a male's testes so that he becomes infertile.

commemorate To celebrate or serve as a memorial.

decommission To take something out of service.

dignitary An individual of high stature or someone who holds a high rank or office.

diplomacy An official relationship between nations.

divine Relating to the gods or the heavens.

eunuch A male who has been castrated.

flotilla Another word for a fleet of ships.

legacy Something left behind after someone dies.

Mecca Located in Saudi Arabia, the holy city of Islam.

Muslim A worshipper of the Islamic religion and follower of the prophet Muhammad.

Persian Resident of Persia, an old state where Iran is today.

porcelain A type of white ceramic.

scribe A writer.

shipwright Someone who builds ships.

tribute A gift given as a show of respect.

Cheng Ho Museum
51 Lorong Hang Jebat 75200
Malacca Town, Malacca, Melaka
Malaysia
Website: http://www.chengho.org/museum/index.html
"Cheng Ho" is the Malaysian name for Zheng He. This
    four-story museum is dedicated to his visits to the
    region. Highlights include models of his ships, a
    wax museum, and audio-visual presentations.

National Geographic
1145 17th Street NW
Washington, DC 20036–4688
(202) 857-7000
Website: http://www.nationalgeographic.com
The world's society of explorers has several articles
    on Zheng He and countless others on the places
    he visited.

Zheng He Park and Zheng He Memorial Hall
26 Zhenghe Road
Kunyang Town, Jinning County
Yunnan Province
China
A 25-hectare (62-acre) park, this memorial garden
    is the final resting place of several of Zheng He's
    relations and includes sculpture, walking grounds,

and a 1,600 square-meter (17,222 square-foot) hall
with displays about the admiral's travels.

Zheng He Treasure Ship Park
No.57 Lijiang Street
Nanjing
China
Website: http://www.bccyz.com
Situated in the same city from which the great admiral
    sailed, this park has a giant replica ship, ancient
    handmade models, maritime history, and lots to do
    for the entire family.

Websites

Because of the changing nature of internet links,
Rosen Publishing has developed an online list of
websites related to the subject of this book. This site
is updated regularly. Please use this link to access
this list:

http://www.rosenlinks.com/SEC/he

Bowle, Ann, and Lak-Khee Tay-Audouard. *Adventures of the Treasure Fleet: China Discovers the World.* Rutland, VT: Tuttle Publishing, 2006.

Brezina, Corona. *Zheng He: China's Greatest Explorer, Mariner, and Navigator.* New York, NY: Rosen Publishing, 2016.

Levathes, Louise. *When China Ruled the Seas: The Treasure Fleet of the Dragon Throne, 1405–1433.* Oxford, England: Oxford University Press, 1997.

Li Jian and Yijin Wert. *Zheng He, the Great Chinese Explorer: A Bilingual Story of Adventure and Discovery.* Shanghai, China: Shanghai Press, 2015.

Song Nan Zhang and Hao Yu Zhang. *The Great Voyages of Zheng He.* Union City, CA: Pan Asian Publications, 2015.

Tong, Tommy, and Michael Blendermann. *Zheng He of China.* Kindle edition. Tommy Tong Publications, 2015.

Wang, Jienan. *Zheng He's Voyages to the Western Oceans.* Beijing, China: China Intercontinental Press, 2010.

Dreyer, Edward L. *Zheng He: China and the Oceans in the Early Ming Dynasty, 1405–1433*. New York, NY: Pearson Education, 2007.

Economist. "China Beat Columbus to It, Perhaps." January 12, 2006. http://www.economist.com/node/5381851.

Ignatius, Adi. "The Asian Voyage: In the Wake of the Admiral." *Time*, August 20, 2001. http://content.time.com/time/world/article/0,8599,2054421,00.html.

Lost Islamic History. "The Muslim Who Was China's Greatest Explorer – Zheng He." Retrieved September 12, 2016. http://lostislamichistory.com/zheng-he.

Murphy, Zoe. "Zheng He: Symbol of China's 'Peaceful Rise.'" BBC, July 28, 2010. http://www.bbc.com/news/world-asia-pacific-10767321.

Rozario, Paul. *Zheng He and the Treasure Fleet, 1405–1433: A Modern Day Traveller's Guide from Antiquity to the Present.* Singapore: SNP International Publishing, 2005.

Viviano, Frank. "China's Great Armada." *National Geographic*, July 2005. http://ngm.nationalgeographic.com/ngm/0507/feature2.

Wade, Geoff. "The Zheng He Voyages: A Reassessment." *Journal of the Malaysian Branch of the Royal Asiatic Society*, 78(1) (288), 37–58. Retrieved September 12, 2016. http://www.jstor.org/stable/41493537.

About the Author

Andrew Vietze is the author or coauthor of ten books, including the Amazon bestseller *Boon Island*, the award-winning biography *Becoming Teddy Roosevelt*, and Rosen Publishing's *Kublai Khan: Emperor of China*. His work has been featured on the Travel Channel and has won multiple awards. A practicer of taiji, Vietze has long had a fascination with the Far East.

Photo Credits